MW01265301

EPHESIANS
LECTIO DIVINA FOR YOUTH

ANCIENT FAITH SERIES

Barefoot Ministries®
Kansas City, Missouri

ISBN 978-0-8341-5028-7

Printed in the United States of America

Written by Ken Heer
Editor: Mike Wonch
Assistant Editor: Catherine M. Shaffer
Cover Design: JR Caines
Interior Design: Sharon Page

Adapted from *Lectio Divina Bible Studies: Listening for God Through Ephesians*.

Heer, Ken. *Lectio Divina Bible Studies: Listening for God Through Ephesians*. Indianapolis, IN: Wesleyan Publishing House and Beacon Hill Press of Kansas City, 2006.

Library of Congress Control Number: 2008934664

10 9 8 7 6 5 4 3 2 1

ABOUT THE *LECTIO DIVINA* BIBLE STUDIES

Lectio divina (pronounced lek-tsee-oh dih-vee-nuh), is a Latin phrase that means *sacred reading*. It is the ancient Christian practice of communicating with God through the reading and study of Scripture. Throughout history, great Christian leaders have used and adapted this ancient method of interpreting Scripture.

The idea behind *lectio divina* is to look at a Bible passage in such a way that Bible study becomes less about study and more about listening. The approach is designed to focus our attention on what God is saying to us through the Word. Through the process of *lectio divina* we not only read to understand with our minds, but we read to hear with our hearts and obey. It is a way of listening to God through His Word.

Some throughout history have said that *lectio divina* turns Bible study on its head—normally we read the Bible, but in *lectio divina, the Bible reads us*. That is probably a good way to describe it. It is God using His Word in a conversation with us to read into our lives and speak to our hearts.

In this series, we will use the traditional *lectio divina* model. We have expanded each component so that it can be used by both individuals and by groups. Each session in this study includes the following elements. (Latin words and their pronunciation are noted in parentheses.)

- **Reading** (*Lectio* "lek-tsee-oh"). We begin with a time of quieting ourselves prior to reading. Then we take a slow, careful reading of a passage of Scripture. We focus our minds on the central theme of the passage. When helpful, we read out loud or read the same passage over and over several times.
- **Meditation** (*Meditatio* "medi-tah-tsee-oh"). Next, we explore the meaning of the Bible passage. Here we dig deep to try to un-

derstand all of what God might be saying to us. We think on the passage. We explore the images, and pay attention to the emotions and feelings that the passage provides. We put ourselves in the story. We look for particular words or phrases that leap off the page as the Spirit begins to speak to us through the Word.

- **Prayer** (*Oratio* "or-ah-tsee-oh"). As we meditate on the passage, we respond to God by communicating with Him. We specifically ask God to speak to us through His Word. We begin to dialog with Him about what we have read. We express praise, thanksgiving, confession, or agreement to God. And we listen. We wait before Him in silence, allowing God the chance to speak.
- **Contemplation** (*Contemplatio* "con-tehm-plah-tsee-oh"). At this point in our conversation through the Word, we come to a place where we rest in the presence of God. Our study is now about receiving what He has said to us. Imagine two old friends who have just talked at length—and now without words, they just sit together and enjoy each other's presence. Having spent time listening to God, we know a little better how God is shaping the direction of our lives. Here there is a yielding of oneself to God's will. We resolve to act on the message of Scripture.

GROUP STUDY

This book is designed to be useful for both individual and group study. To use this in a group, you may take one of several approaches:

- **Individual Study/Group Review**. Make sure each member of the group has a copy of the book. Have them read through one section during the week. (They will work through the same passage or portions of it each day that week.) Then, when you meet together, review what thoughts, notes, and insights the members of the group experienced in their individual study. Use the group questions at the end of the section as a guide.
- **Group Lectio**. Make sure each member of the group has a copy of the book. Have them read through one section during the

week in individual study. When you meet together as a group, you will study the passage together through a reading form similar to lectio divina:

- **First, read the passage out loud several times to the group.** Group members respond by waiting in silence and letting God speak.
- **Second, have the passage read aloud again to the group once or twice more.** Use different group members for different voices, and have them read slowly. Group members listen for a word or two that speaks to them, and share it with the group. Break into smaller groups if appropriate.
- **Third, read the passage out loud again, and have the group pray together to ask God what He might be saying to each person, and to the group as a whole.** Go around and share what each person is learning from this process. At this point, review together the group questions at the end of the section.[1]

- **Lectio Divina Steps for Groups.** Make sure each member has a copy of the book. As a group, move through the study together, going through each of the parts: reading, meditation, prayer, and contemplation. Be sure to use the group questions at the end of the section.

The important thing about using *lectio divina* in a group is to remember that this is to be incarnational ("in the flesh")—in other words, we begin to live out the Word in our community. We carry God's Word in us, (in the flesh, or incarnate in us) and we carry that Word into our group to be lived out among them.

The *Lectio Divina Bible Studies* invite readers to slow down, read Scripture, meditate upon it, and prayerfully respond to God's Word.

---

1. Parts of the "Group Lectio" section adapted from Tony Jones, *The Sacred Way: Spiritual Practices for Everyday Life,* Grand Rapids: Zondervan, 2005, p. 54.

CONTENTS

INTRODUCTION

In the Book of Ephesians, God's children are called to heavenly living in a less-than-heavenly world. God has "raised us up with Christ and seated us with him in heavenly realms" (2:6). While we have a new life in Christ and a new relationship with God that is filled with new blessings, we continue to live in our old-world environment—dominated by "the ways of this world" and under the influence of "the spirit who is now at work in those who are disobedient" (2:2).

This book was written to a group of believers in the city of Ephesus whom Paul had helped to come to faith in Christ. The founding of that church is recorded in Acts 16.

Ephesus was a Greek city under Roman occupation. The city had become a religious, political, and commercial center. The people had been influenced by the immorality and idolatries of paganism (a pagan temple dedicated to the Roman goddess Diana was located in Ephesus). In light of this, it was essential that believers there be assured of their doctrine[2], their position in Christ, and their defenses against attacks on their faith.

---

2. Doctrine is the teaching that is accepted by member of a religion. Christian doctrine is the set of beliefs about God as accepted by Christians. (Eby, J. Wesley, ed., *A Dictionary of the Bible & Christian Doctrine in Everyday English*. Kansas City: Beacon Hill Press of Kansas City, 2004., p. 80)

With this need in clear view, the text lifts us into the heights of doctrinal truth and spiritual blessing, and then plunges us into the day-to-day experience of applying that doctrine in the realities of life in this world. It prepares us for the reality of living with the challenge of being in Christ and in the world.

Paul describes and defines our position in Christ with words such as the following: *glorious, incomparable, immeasurable, unsearchable, manifold, surpassing, lavished*—all used in connection with the blessings God has bestowed upon us in heavenly realms so we can live effectively in earthly realms.

As you meditate upon God's Word to believers living in an unbelieving culture, allow Him to help you see the timeless truths needed for you to remain vital in your connection to Christ and vibrant in your witness.

The apostle Paul wrote this letter that you might be assured of your position in Christ, aware of your privileges, armed against the powers and principalities of this world, and able to live with a little bit of heaven on earth.

LIVING IN GOD'S BLESSINGS

LISTENING FOR GOD THROUGH EPHESIANS 1:3-23

SUMMARY

God is the Great Initiator. He begins things in our lives that we are incapable of beginning ourselves. Anything good in our world and in our lives finds its origin and completion in God. He has a purpose and a plan for everything and everyone, including you. Life begins and ends with Him.

Grace is God's agent for accomplishing His purpose and plan in human lives. It is the favor of God that is undeserved and unearned, a gift given freely with the only condition that it is received by faith. God enjoys lavishing His grace on those who place their faith in Him.

Because of our sin, we are by nature outside of God's saving grace and separated from His spiritual life. Through Christ, though, we can be chosen by God, forgiven of our sins, adopted into His spiritual family, included in His blessings, and guaranteed an eternal inheritance.

God's plan is for you to become His child and enjoy the blessings of life in Christ. Are you ready to step into His blessings?

PREPARATION ☦ Focus Your Thoughts

Do you know what it means to be excluded from a group or a benefit enjoyed by others? On the other hand, what does it feel like to be chosen?

What do you consider to be the greatest benefit of being chosen to be in God's family?

READING ☦ Hear the Word

Many people consider the study of doctrine to be disinteresting and disconnected from real life. In this section of Scripture, Paul presents the doctrine of salvation in terms that connect with us in a meaningful way. You will come across some terms that are rich with meaning. Here are a few of them:

> *Chosen:* The Jews were called God's chosen people. In Christ you, too, are one of His chosen.
>
> *Adopted:* Being adopted into the family of God, with all of its benefits, is a result of being chosen.
>
> *Predestined:* God had you in mind before you knew Him. In Christ, He decided He wanted you to be a part of His eternal family. He is even now at work in your

life, encouraging you to respond to His offer of grace.

Forgiven: Only God is able to remove the guilt of your sin and the judgment that is against it. In Christ, God frees you from sin's penalty.

Inheritance: Because you have been forgiven and adopted into God's family, you have a guaranteed eternal inheritance—a heavenly home where you will be with God and all other redeemed persons.

With these terms in mind, prayerfully read Ephesians 1:3-23.

MEDITATION ✝ ENGAGE THE WORD

Meditate on Ephesians 1:3-8

Verse 3 says God has blessed us "with every spiritual blessing." In what ways has God blessed you? Verses 4-8 describe some of the spiritual blessings available in Christ. What meaning does each of these blessings carry in your life?

Verse 4 says it is God's intent that we be "holy and blameless." What does this mean? How does a person become holy?

Read the quote by Keith Drury on page 16. He says the *condition* of holiness results from the *activity* of sanctification. Where do you find the word *sanctification* in the Scriptures? What do you understand it to mean?

> *We become holy—Christlike—through sanctification . . . Sanctification is God's Spirit at work in my mind, soul, spirit, body—my entire life—changing and renewing my desires, thoughts, interests, attitudes, and behaviors.*
>
> *—Keith Drury*

Meditate on Ephesians 1:9-14

These verses indicate that the will of God involves His purpose, plan, and pleasure. What is the meaning of each of these?

Read the Roman proverb below. Do you have a good sense of what God's purpose is for your life? Are you accepting His plan so the winds that come your way will move you toward the destination God has for you?

> *When the pilot does not know what port he is heading for, no wind is the right wind. —Roman Proverb*

Verse 13 says that in Christ you were included. On what basis have you now been included? How would you describe your feelings about being included?

Meditate on Ephesians 1:15-23

In these verses we gain a glimpse inside the heart of Paul and especially into his prayer life. What does he say about his relationship with the people in Ephesus?

When he tells them he remembers them in his prayers, what specific things does he say he includes in his prayer? Which of these things would you most like someone to pray for you?

Verse 23 speaks of "the fullness of him who fills everything in every way." What do you think Paul means by *fullness?* In what ways does God fill everything in every way?

A. W. Tozer said the fullness of God refers to His self-sufficiency: He needs nothing to complete himself, and He is never diminished. Read the Tozer quote. In what ways must you find your sufficiency in Him who alone is fully self-sufficient?

> *The river grows larger by its tributaries, but where is the tributary that can enlarge the One out of whom came everything and to whose infinite fullness all creation owes its being?*
>
> *—A. W. Tozer*

Read the quote on page 18 about St. Theresa's confidence in the ability of God. This is consistent with verse 19, where Paul says the "incomparably great power" of God is at work on your behalf. How has the power of God been demonstrated recently in your life? When would you have been sunk without His help?

St. Theresa once wanted to build an orphanage but she had only three shillings. Someone jeeringly said to her, "What can you do to build an orphanage with only three shillings?" She replied, "Theresa with three shillings, can do nothing, but with three shillings and with God to help there is nothing that Theresa cannot do!"

PRAYER ✝ ASK AND LISTEN

Seek the face of God. Ask, "Lord, what are You saying to us today?"

Paul said God chose you to be the beneficiary of His spiritual blessings and to "sit with Christ in heavenly realms." Are you enjoying the blessings that are promised you as a child of God?

Pray that all of the spiritual blessings of Christ may be fully released and realized in you.

CONTEMPLATION ✝ REFLECT AND YIELD

Is the redemptive purpose of God being fully realized in your life?

How can you trace the plan of God unfolding in your life?

Group Study

- What is your definition of holiness? How did you arrive at this definition?

- How is holiness demonstrated in your life?

- Are there compartments of your mind, soul, spirit, and body where you know God is acting presently to sanctify you?

- How will your life be different this week in light of the blessings you have in Christ?

- Are you relying on the sufficiency of God? If not, how could you change this?

- Do you have someone who is praying with and for you? If not, think about who you could ask to be your prayer partner.

LIVING A TRANSFORMED LIFE

LISTENING FOR GOD THROUGH EPHESIANS 2:1-22

Summary

The best way to see the changes that have occurred in a person or place is to have before and after pictures—a comparison of the present with the past. In matters of faith it is much the same. The grace of God, extended in Christ and activated through the presence and power of the Holy Spirit, transforms us so that we are not what we once were.

Some changes that have happened in your life may be obvious to you and to those who know you. These outward, visible changes are the result of a transformation in the kind of person you are now on the inside—your nature has been changed.

Paul says God has not only forgiven you and adopted you into His forever family, but He has transformed (and will continue to transform) your nature as He builds a temple for His Spirit inside you.

PREPARATION ☩ Focus Your Thoughts

What has changed about you since you accepted Christ? Do you like the person you have become?

If you could change something else about yourself, what would it be?

READING ☩ Hear the Word

Paul is writing to first-generation believers—people who came to Christ out of paganism. Ephesus was a place where many different religions converged and were often intermingled with idolatry, witchcraft, and immorality.

It is impossible to embrace Christ while continuing to embrace pagan practices. When people come to Christ, their way of living must change. But practices can become habits that are hard to change. Something fundamental to the nature of a person must be changed for habitual behavior to be changed.

Read Ephesians 2:1-22. As you do, note how these verses give a picture of what you used to be and how God has changed you so you are capable of living a transformed life.

MEDITATION ✝ Engage the Word

Meditate on Ephesians 2:1-3

Paul described the pre-Christian life as being dead in transgressions and sins. In what ways were you dead before you came to Christ?

Paul also said that the "ways of this world" influence the way people live. What are these "ways," and how do they impact behavior?

Read the quote from comedian Fred Allen. Why is that way of living both dangerous and displeasing to God?

> *Most of us spend the first six days of each week sowing wild oats; then we go to church on Sunday and pray for a crop failure.* —*Fred Allen*

Paul indicates that the way we used to live was influenced by our sins, the ways of the world, the evil spirit that is at work, and our sinful nature. He says our sinful nature has cravings, desires, and thoughts that make up a nature in us that is displeasing to God. In what areas of your own life have you felt the displeasure of God?

Meditate on Ephesians 2:4-10

Our *after* picture is much better to look at than our *before* picture. It is made possible because of God's love, mercy, and grace. How have you experienced God's love, mercy, and grace in your life?

We were "dead in transgressions;" now we are "alive with Christ." When we are saved, God raises us up. What does it mean to you that God has raised you up?

Grace is the most optimistic thing in the world. It says that anyone can be changed. It offers hope for this life and the one to come. There is nothing we are or can do to deserve salvation—it is a gift of grace. What are some ways people try to earn salvation?

Verse 10 says you are now the special object of God's creation. He is working on you. He is preparing you for something good. In what areas of your life are you conscious that God has been at work? What are some good works that you sense God is preparing you to do?

Read the quote of William Jordan. Who are the people most influenced by your transformed life?

> *Into the hands of every individual is given a marvelous power for good or evil—the silent, unconscious, unseen influence of his life.* —*William George Jordan*

Meditate on Ephesians 2:11-20

Circumcision was an outward, physical act to which male Jews submitted as a sign of their identification with Jehovah God. By birth Gentiles were uncircumcised outsiders—separated foreigners to God's covenant with Israel. What was God's purpose in having a chosen people? How did this outward sign indicate an inner commitment?

Verse 12 says we were once "without God" and "without hope." Who are some people you know who live without God and without hope? In what ways do their lives demonstrate this reality?

In verse 12, Paul asks the Ephesian believers to remember their former lives. While there may be things of our past that we are ashamed of and would just as soon forget, it may be helpful to occasionally remember how life used to be when we were separated and excluded.

Verse 13 says it is through the blood of Christ that we have been included within God's covenant and blessing. Verse 16 says the Cross has been the agent of reconciling everyone, regardless of nationality, to God. Why was the death of Christ necessary?

Verse 18 says that through Christ we have "access to the Father." What does this mean? How are you taking advantage of this privilege?

Meditate on Ephesians 2:21-22

These verses have both corporate and individual meaning. The people of God as a community come together as a "holy temple in the Lord." God has chosen to dwell with and demonstrate His presence through the Church—the community of believers. How have you witnessed the presence and power of God within your church?

Read the quote from Bill Bright. Compare it to verse 22 where Paul says the Spirit of God seeks to dwell in you as a person. There is some building going on inside you so you can be a fit dwelling place for God. Where has He had to do some demolition? What improvements has He made since He has come to live inside you?

> *To be filled with the Holy Spirit is to be filled with Christ. . . If I am controlled and empowered by Christ, He will be walking around in my body, living His resurrection life in and through me.* —*Bill Bright*

PRAYER ✝ ASK AND LISTEN

Seek the face of God. Ask, "Lord, what are You saying to us today?"

The grace of God through Christ changes our relationship and standing with God as it changes the kind of people we are. How has grace changed you? Where is God at work in you right now?

Pray silently, thanking God for including you in His family and asking Him to show you any area of your life that needs to be changed.

CONTEMPLATION ☦ Reflect and Yield

Are you comfortable with the realization that you are a temple for God to live in? Are there specific areas of your life that you have had difficulty yielding to the transforming work of God?

What might be different in your life if you were "filled with the Spirit"?

Group Study

- How would you describe what it is like to be alive with Christ?
- What is one area of pressure you experience from the "ways of this world"? In what ways would you like God to help you the next time you face that pressure?

- On what basis might people think they deserve salvation? Why is this contrary to what God's Word says?

- Think about how your life used to be before you had Christ in your life. How is your life changed now that you have a relationship with Him?

- How does having the hope of God make a difference in your life?

- We are witnesses to the changes God has brought into our lives through our word and actions—what we say and what we do. Make a list of three people to whom you can tell your before-and-after story during the next two weeks.

LIVING IN THE PURPOSE AND POWER OF GOD

LISTENING FOR GOD THROUGH EPHESIANS 3:1-21

SUMMARY

God has a purpose for the world and for your life. He has a plan that He is working out that will fulfill His purpose. Some moments it may appear as if God is not in control, but He has an intent, a purpose, and a plan that are demonstrated in the flow of history. It is in knowing the purpose God has for you and experiencing the power of God within you that you discover how to experience and maintain an earth-bound life with a bit of heaven in it. Your personal courage and conviction will grow out of the belief that you are being and doing what God intends.

Paul had a good grip on his purpose in life. His purpose was inextricably intertwined with God's purpose. His work in the world was a part of God's plan.

Yet having a purpose and a plan is not enough. You must have the power to carry out your purpose and plan, or they are only empty rhetoric and unrealistic dreams. God not only has power beyond your imagination to carry out His purpose and plan, but that power is at work in you to help fulfill your life's purpose and engage yourself effectively in God's plan.

PREPARATION ☦ FOCUS YOUR THOUGHTS

How is God working in the world? What do you believe to be His purpose for your life?

READING ☦ HEAR THE WORD

The apostle Paul was on a mission from God to make plain to everyone God's purpose for humankind. At times, it might have appeared to be a mystery as to what God was up to. The mission of Paul was to proclaim that the gospel—the Good News—was for everyone, Jew or Gentile. His purpose was to be sure others understood the purpose of God and lived within the blessings of His grace.

Paul was clear in this purpose. In this passage, he refers to himself as "the prisoner of Christ" and "a servant of the gospel." Both *prisoner* and *servant* might be considered demeaning and restrictive. Did Paul behave as if either were true?

Another of Paul's wonderful prayers is recorded in this passage. He prays that the power of God would be experienced in the lives of these believers so they would be strengthened in their "inner being." Many people who have the power of physique, position, and possessions ultimately fall and fail in life, because they are weak on the inside.

Consider these thoughts as you read Ephesians 3:1-21.

MEDITATION ✝ Engage the Word

Meditate on Ephesians 3:1-6

Paul had a clear sense that he was living out a mission assignment from God. What brought him to this conviction?

The purpose of Paul's life included bringing a message and blessing to others. Do you view your purpose to include a similar mission?

Read the explanation by Ray Stedman of the mystery mentioned by Paul. Who around you is in desperate need of knowing God's "sacred secrets"?

> *The "mysteries" are the sacred secrets that God knows about life, which men desperately need to know.*
>
> *—Ray Stedman*

Meditate on Ephesians 3:7-12

Paul viewed himself to be the least likely, least-deserving person to be called by God with such an important purpose. Because of grace and the transforming, enabling power of God, however, he fulfilled his purpose. When have you felt inadequate and less than the least?

Read the quote by Rick Warren. God is the source of our purpose. What He has in mind for you, He has the power to make happen. Do you have the conviction that regardless of your inadequacies and your circumstances, God is working in you and through you to accomplish His purpose?

> *The purpose of your life is far greater than your own personal fulfillment, your peace of mind, or even your happiness. It's far greater than your family, your career, or even your wildest dreams and ambitions. If you want to know why you were placed on this planet, you must begin with God. You were born by His purpose and for His purpose.* —*Rick Warren*

A part of God's plan is that you have access to His presence, as well as His power. He wants you to approach Him with freedom and confidence. How might this have been a new idea to the readers of this letter?

Meditate on Ephesians 3:13-21

Prayer was a vital part of Paul's relationship with God and of his care about the needs of his friends. He was experiencing suffering, but his prayer for others reflected his reliance upon God for his own adequacy, as well as theirs. Recall times when you've been in your own difficult times, but you carried others to God in prayer. How did praying for others affect you during those times?

Read the quote from Sherwood Eddy. Can you say that you live with "spiritual power"? If not, how can you?

> *We readily admit that Jesus and all the genuine saints throughout history had spiritual power and that they had a deep prayer life. We believe that there must be some connection between their power and their life of prayer.* —*Sherwood Eddy*

Verse 16 indicates that our greatest need is for strength in our "inner being." What do you understand this to mean? What is the source of this strengthening?

The words *dwell, rooted,* and *established* in verse 17 speak of permanence and stability. What connection is there between these words as they appear in this passage?

Grasping the dimensions of the love of Christ is a major focus of this prayer. How wide is the love of Christ? How long? How high? How deep? What have you come to understand about this love that exceeds understanding?

Living with a bit of heaven on earth is possible as you live within the purpose, plan, and power of God. What does Paul say regarding God's ability to accomplish this in verse 20?

PRAYER ☩ ASK AND LISTEN

Seek the face of God. Ask, "Lord, what are You saying to us today?"

Read the statement below about prayer. Tell God about your inadequacies, fears, and questions. Experience His mercy and grace flowing into your spirit. He is at work within you and is able to do more than you could ask or imagine. Experience His love and His fullness.

> *Our prayer and God's mercy are like two buckets in a well; while the one ascends the other descends.*
>
> *—Mark Hopkins*

CONTEMPLATION ☩ REFLECT AND YIELD

Do you understand the purpose God has for you? How are you living out that purpose? Are you ready to follow God's purpose wherever it may take you and do whatever it may call you to do?

Group Study

- If God could do something in your life that you are incapable of doing yourself, what do you think it might be?

- Can you identify someone in your life who has brought grace, hope, and blessing to you? Take time to think of ways to thank them this week.

- What is your responsibility for giving insights into the mystery of the gospel to those who need to know?

- How has God helped you carry out His plan for you despite your weaknesses and inadequacies?

- How do we fellowship with an awesome and holy God?

- God wants each of us to be servants of the gospel, helping to spread the word about what He is up to in the world. How can you share the Good News at your school this week? Is there a person God brings to your mind who needs to hear the gospel?

LIVING IN A LOVING, GROWING COMMUNITY

LISTENING FOR GOD THROUGH EPHESIANS 4:1-16

SUMMARY

Christians do not try to make it in the world on their own. They come to Christ one person at a time, but from that moment on, they are a part of a larger community. You can find that family of faith anywhere you go in the world. Believers are bound together with common faith, common life, common values, and common purpose.

The family of God takes the shape of a local church community. The church was God's invention for the spiritual stability and growth of His people. It is within the church community that you celebrate your oneness with Christ, you are gifted for service, and you receive the nurture and discipline necessary to mature spiritually.

Living so you experience a bit of heaven on earth will be enhanced through the fellowship, encouragement, and challenge to your spiritual maturity that results from being a part of a local church family.

PREPARATION ☩ FOCUS YOUR THOUGHTS

Think of a special time that your church really supported you and demonstrated Christ's love to you. What is the present status of your relationship with a local church family?

READING ☩ HEAR THE WORD

Paul has laid the foundation of doctrinal truths and spiritual blessings upon which the readers' faith has been built. He now turns his attention to the importance of relationships within the community of people who have accepted Christ. He tells them about the common things that are bonds between them.

He tells them God has selected persons for leadership within the church and has gifted them to enable all members of the community to serve each other and to serve God in the world. He tells them the church is to be a loving community where people are motivated to grow into spiritual maturity.

With these truths in mind, read Ephesians 4:1-16.

MEDITATION ☩ ENGAGE THE WORD

Meditate on Ephesians 4:1-6

Paul is writing from a Roman prison. However, in none of his writings does he indicate that prison has defeated him or stripped him of his ability to carry out the purpose of his life. In fact, in verse 1 he says he is a "prisoner for the Lord." He is not a prisoner of Rome, but a prisoner for the Lord. What does he mean by this? How could this perspective modify his mood and mission?

Read the quote from *Brotherhood Journal.* Is there one person in particular who you think of when you read this? Are there people with whom you disagree, but with whom you wish to walk arm in arm?

> *Christians may not see eye to eye, but they can walk arm in arm.* —Brotherhood Journal

One of the evidences of God's work in people is how they feel toward, and get along with, each other. What virtues characterize Christian community life in verses 2 and 3?

The unity of the church finds its origin in the oneness of God and His salvation plan. Read the statement on page 40 by J. I. Packer regarding the mystery of the Trinity (God the Father, Son, and Holy Spirit). It is difficult for us to wrap our minds around the possibility of three distinct persons of one essential nature. Yet this doctrinal truth is at the heart of our faith. Sometimes it is just as difficult for us to wrap our arms around people who are different and difficult, yet this is at the heart of our faith community. Unity is an expression of the presence and power of God. Where He is, there is unity. How can you begin to express unity in a new way in your church community?

> *Here are two mysteries for the price of one—the plurality of persons within the unity of God, and the union of Godhead and manhood in the person of Jesus.*
>
> —*J. I. Packer*

Meditate on Ephesians 4:7-11

God's grace is offered to everyone as a means of salvation. This grace is also at work in every person who is in Christ, transforming them and preparing them for the purpose God has for them. Grace comes in the shape of gifts—talents, spiritual abilities, opportunities, and positions. Paul identified several specific leadership positions for which persons had been gifted—apostles, prophets, evangelist, and pastors/teachers. What do you understand these different positions to be? Are there modern counterparts to these positions? What do they look like?

Meditate on Ephesians 4:12-16

According to verse 12, the purpose for the functioning of those with leadership gifts is "to prepare God's people for works of service." Is this your view of the purpose of leaders in your church—to prepare *you* for service? Are hired leaders the only ones responsible to do the work of the church?

The huge redwood trees in California are the tallest trees in the world and some are over 2,500 years old. They have a shallow system of roots, but their roots all intertwine. They are locked to each other, and do not stand alone, for all the trees support and protect each other. What application of this fact can you make to the nature and function of the church?

God's plan is that all of His children would be engaged in service so the "body of Christ may be built up" and "become mature."

In verse 12 the church is referred to as the "body of Christ." What other images are used in the Scripture to portray the nature and function of the church? Which imagery is the most meaningful to you?

What are the indicators of immaturity as expressed in verse 14? What are the indicators of maturity as expressed in verses 15-16?

Do you agree with the statement by Augustine on page 42? What results when Christians neglect a strong attachment to a church where they can experience meaningful, loving relationships?

He cannot have God for his Father who refuses to have the church for his mother. —*Augustine*

Living with a bit of heaven on earth is dependant upon being a part of a loving, growing community of believers. Is that how you would describe your church family? What contribution are you making to help make your church a place where people are loved and where they can mature in their Christian faith?

Read Jane Howard's statement. Does this apply to a universal need for the church? Is your need for the church being adequately met? Is the need of others being met by what you contribute to the family of God?

Call it a clan, call it a network, call it a tribe, call it a family. Whatever you call it, whoever you are, you need one. —*Jane Howard*

PRAYER ✝ ASK AND LISTEN

Seek the face of God. Ask, "Lord, what are You saying to us today?"

God has gifted people to give leadership to your church. Do

you regularly support them with prayer, respect, and affirmation?

Pray that God will strengthen your church by blessing your leaders and by calling workers who are willing to get engaged in service. Listen for His promptings for how you can serve.

CONTEMPLATION ✝ Reflect and Yield

How has God gifted you for serving in and through the church? What area of ministry in your church presently needs help? If God opens an opportunity for you to serve in that area, would you be willing to accept it?

Group Study

- Believers have received a calling of which they are to live worthy. What is this calling, and how does a person live up to it?

- If there is one thing you could do within the church that would help others grow, what would it be?

- Are you contributing to the unity of the church? If so, how? If not, how might you become involved in building the unity?

- How does involvement in service contribute to growth and maturity?

- Make a list of the characteristics you think should exist in a mature Christian. On a scale of one to five—five being highest—rate yourself on each of the characteristics. What can you begin today that will stimulate spiritual growth in the area in which you need it most?

LIVING A HOLY LIFE

LISTENING FOR GOD THROUGH EPHESIANS 4:17-32

SUMMARY

God calls us to himself so we can be transformed and live a new life that has Jesus Christ as its pattern. He calls us so that He can accomplish His purposes for us as we cooperate with Him.

One of those purposes, which Paul identified back in chapter 1, is that we be "holy and blameless." Holy living involves how we think, how we express our attitudes, how we speak, and how we behave toward others. There is no part of our life that should remain outside of God's cleansing, transforming work. This holy living requires empowerment by God's Spirit alongside full commitment on our part. God will not violate the free expression of our choice; we have to exercise our decision to put our faith in His forgiving and cleansing power.

The goal of your life should be to become more and more like Jesus. He was kind, compassionate, and forgiving. When you live like Him, you help bring these gifts to others.

PREPARATION ☨ FOCUS YOUR THOUGHTS

Can you recall a time recently when you were made aware that the way you think and behave is radically different than those in the non-Christian world? How did you react to this difference? Did it make you feel different and odd, or did it affirm your commitment to Christ and cause you to feel encouraged?

READING ☨ HEAR THE WORD

As difficult as it may be sometimes, when we become followers of Christ we are to be changed people who live differently than we did before. In fact, God asks that we be holy as He is holy. This requires radical changes in us.

Every change we need may not happen overnight, but we need to commit ourselves to becoming individuals who reflect the work of God that is going on within us as He makes us Christlike.

Look for the characteristics Paul gives to those he calls Gentiles. Do any of these characteristics describe you before you became a Christian? Do they describe any of the people you see around you? What is to be your response to your "former way of life"? Consider those questions as you read Ephesians 4:17-32.

MEDITATION ✝ Engage the Word

Meditate on Ephesians 4:17-19

Our behavior grows out of how we think and how we view our world. Gentiles, or unbelievers, are characterized as being futile in their thinking. What does Paul mean by this? In what way is the thinking of unbelievers futile?

Read the Oswald Sanders quote. How are his comments consistent with verse 18, which speaks of darkened understanding, ignorance, and hardening of the heart? How is this reflected in the thinking of an unbeliever?

> *The mind of man is the battleground on which every moral and spiritual battle is fought.*
>
> *—J. Oswald Sanders*

Meditate on Ephesians 4:20-24

Most of us are indebted to someone for telling (teaching) us about Jesus. Who have been the great teachers in your life who have both taught you about Jesus and shown you what it means to follow Him?

Verse 22 says we are to put off our old self. What do you understand that to mean? How do you do it?

Verse 23 says we are to have a new attitude and a new mind. How has your way of thinking and your attitude toward life changed since you have become a new creature in Christ?

Read the comment about Mahatma Gandhi. We are to become new persons who are to live like Jesus and are created to be like God. He is characterized as being righteous and holy. What do you understand this to mean?

> *Missionary E. Stanley Jones once asked Mahatma Gandhi how Christianity could be more acceptable in India. His reply was, "I would suggest, first, that all of you Christians . . . begin to live more like Jesus."*

Meditate on Ephesians 4:25-28

Holy living involves how we relate to others. It is as basic as being honest and truthful.

Read the quote from *The Baptist Beacon* on page 49. At some point in most people's lives, they have a problem with anger. Paul says when we are angry we should not sin. What does he mean by this? Do you suppose it has something to do with the acid effect of anger?

> *Anger is an acid that can do more harm to the vessel in which it is stored than to anything on which it is poured.* —The Baptist Beacon

According to verses 26-27, what is a Christian's responsibility regarding anger? How can expressing anger give the devil a foothold?

Likewise, Paul reminds us in verse 28 that Christians should be engaged in honest labor. Not only should this result in doing beneficial things for others, but also in gaining resources that can be shared with those who are needy. How does this differ from the work motives of many people?

Meditate on Ephesians 4:29-32

As he continues to bring up outward evidences of the new life, Paul reminds us of the power words have to hurt or help others. What kind of talk would you consider to be unwholesome? How can the words you speak build up other people?

Verse 30 says we should not grieve the Holy Spirit. What does this mean? How can a person grieve the Holy Spirit?

Bitterness, rage, anger, brawling, slander, and malice are inconsistent with holy living. Have you ever struggled with any of these?

These verses closely connect our relationship with God and our relationship with others—one affects the other. In what ways should your relationship with God affect your relationship with others? Why would your relationship with others affect your relationship with God?

Persons who are living a holy life should demonstrate kindness and compassion toward others. This may involve forgiving those who wrong you, which is to be done as freely and completely as God has forgiven you. Read the quote from Hannah More. Do you agree with her statement? Why, or why not?

> *A Christian will find it cheaper to pardon than to resent. Forgiveness saves the expense of anger, the cost of hatred, the waste of spirits. —Hannah More*

PRAYER ✝ ASK AND LISTEN

Seek the face of God. Ask, "Lord, what are You saying to us today?"

Salvation is more than being forgiven of your sins. It is being freed from the power sin had over your attitudes and behavior. How has sin's control over you changed since you became a Christian?

Pray and ask God to show you things in your life He wants to cleanse you from, so He can more completely fill you with His Spirit.

Contemplation ✝ Reflect and Yield

In what areas of your life do you still struggle spiritually? Are you willing to let God expose things in you with which He is not pleased?

Group Study

- Are you happy with the changes God is bringing to your life? Is there a particular area in which you know you need more changing?
- What were the characteristics of your old self? What are the characteristics of your new self?
- What does it mean "to be like God in true righteousness and holiness"?
- Why is it hard to forgive some people? Are there persons in your life toward whom you find it difficult to be kind and compassionate? Are there persons you have difficulty forgiving?

- Jesus said the great commandment was to love God with our entire being and to love others as ourselves. Holy living is relational—involving God and others. It requires us to be kind, compassionate, and forgiving—just like Jesus. Is there anyone who needs your forgiveness? What will you do about it today?

LIVING IN LOVE AND LIGHT

LISTENING FOR GOD THROUGH EPHESIANS 5:1-20

SUMMARY

We are most like God when we love others. There are several types of love mentioned in Scripture—each using a different word in the language of the New Testament. There is a word that means family love—the love of a parent for a child. There is a word that means physical, sensual love. There is a word that means friendship love—the bond that exists between people who like to be together. None of these words adequately defines the love God has for us and the love He wants us to have for each other. So a new word appears in the New Testament. This word (*agape*) describes love like God's that caused Him to give His Son for our salvation. That's the kind of love He wants to give us for others.

In another vivid image Paul tells us to live in the light. In Scripture, the light is truth that makes clear the difference between good and evil. It is the Holy Spirit exposing the truth about a matter. We are to bring everything to the light of the Scriptures and the Spirit to test its rightness.

The images of love and light can bring us to a fresher understanding of the life God wants us to experience on earth.

PREPARATION ☨ FOCUS YOUR THOUGHTS

Whom do you admire, and how would you like to be like them?

Have people told you that you look like or have some of the characteristics of other members of your family? How does that make you feel?

READING ☨ HEAR THE WORD

Children carry family traits and often imitate the attitudes and behaviors of their parents. They learn to respond to life through the closeness of their relationships. In the same way, by choice and by close relationship, true children of God imitate their Father.

Looking to Christ as our example, we see first a pattern for living a life of love. Verse 2 says love caused Him to give himself up for us. For many people, love is a means of satisfying emotional needs and gratifying self-centered desires. That leads to the perversion and abuse of love. Following Jesus' example, Christians are conscious of how they relate to others.

Christians follow Christ's example by giving up a life that is dominated by the ways of the world and sinful desires. They live under the powerful influence of the Holy Spirit, whom they have allowed to fill them.

Read Ephesians 5:1-20, and allow these verses to cause you to consider how you can live in the light.

MEDITATION ☩ Engage the Word

Meditate on Ephesians 5:1-2

As Bernard of Clairvaux says, children are deeply influenced by the people they view to be important. They often consciously imitate them. They may even unconsciously pattern themselves after these persons, repeating observed behaviors and attitudes. Children of God are to imitate God, consciously choosing to have their behavior and attitudes shaped by Him. How are you imitating your Heavenly Father?

> *What we love we shall grow to resemble.*
>
> *—Bernard of Clairvaux*

As Henry Ward Beecher states on page 56, the love and sacrifice of Christ is to be our pattern. In what way does your life of love demonstrate itself sacrificially?

We never know how much one loves till we know how much he is willing to endure and suffer for us; and it is the suffering element that measures love.

—Henry Ward Beecher

Meditate on Ephesians 5:3-7

The influence of some people should be avoided. Are there people you have learned are a bad influence on you? How have your friendships changed since you became a Christian?

Read the definition of sin by Walter Carson. Our nature is to distort and pervert the creation of God. How might sexual immorality, impurity, and greed be cheap imitations and perversions of love? Verse 3 says these are improper for God's holy people. How do Christians come to know what is proper and improper?

Sin is twisting and distorting out of its proper shape a human personality which God designed to be a thing of beauty and joy forever. *—Walter Carson*

Paul says out-of-place speaking includes obscenity, foolish talk, and coarse joking. How would you describe the meaning of each of these? What adjectives would you use to characterize your speech?

Verse 5 says immoral, impure, and greedy people are idolaters. How is this so?

The love of God is a major focus of the Book of Ephesians, but on a couple of occasions, like in verse 6, Paul speaks of the wrath of God. How do you reconcile the love of God with the wrath of God? Can He be a loving God and also send His wrath upon people—even cut them off from an eternal inheritance?

Meditate on Ephesians 5:8-14

Verse 8 contrasts our life before Christ with our life after Christ as being as different as darkness and light. Earlier, Paul said our life without Christ was death. Now he says it was darkness. How is life without Christ like living in darkness?

We are to live as children of light. What do you understand this to mean?

Read the statement about conscience by Tryon Edwards. Are you making your conscience a reliable guide?

> *Conscience is merely our own judgment of the right or wrong of our actions, and so can never be a safe guide unless enlightened by the word of God.*
>
> *—Tryon Edwards*

Light exposes secret things and makes things visible. Where do believers go to find the light that exposes potential problems in their lives?

Living with goodness, righteousness, and truth frees a person from the fear of having something discovered that might be embarrassing. In what areas of your life are you proving that you have nothing to hide?

Meditate on Ephesians 5:15-20

Christianity is not just a matter of belief. It is also a matter of behavior. Christians live carefully and wisely. What does that mean in practical terms?

Verse 17 says we are to "understand what the Lord's will is." People often struggle with God's will, either because they don't know what it is or they know and are resisting it. Within the context of these verses, what can you understand about God's will for you?

How does the quote from Paul Little help you put verse 17 into a clear light?

> *Has it ever struck you that the vast majority of the will of God for your life has already been revealed in the Bible?*
>
> *—Paul Little*

Paul encourages the readers to be "filled with the Spirit." What do you understand this to mean? How does a person become filled with the Spirit?

Living in love and light brings joy to a person's spirit. This joy escapes the believer's spirit in the form of uplifting speech and spiritual music. Christians love to sing. The music of their mouths comes from the music in their hearts.

The Book of Acts records that Paul and Silas sang songs at midnight when in prison. Scripture says that when Jesus and the disciples left the Upper Room, and Jesus headed toward the agony of Gethsemane and of Calvary, He led them in singing a song. Has God put a song in your heart that keeps your spirit warm even when the cold winds of adversity are blowing?

PRAYER ✝ Ask and Listen

Seek the face of God. Ask, "Lord, what are You saying to us today?"

We are asked to live in love and light. We are to love sacrificially. We are to live carefully and wisely. We are to be filled with the Spirit and have a song in our hearts. Ask God to help these traits and actions become a reality in your life today. Let His Spirit occupy all of your being and compose the music of heaven in your heart.

CONTEMPLATION ☩ REFLECT AND YIELD

Scriptures makes it clear that some things are compatible with the Christian life. However, not everything in our world is black and white. Christians need to be discerning and able to find out what pleases God and what doesn't. Are there convictions you have developed based on your sense of what pleases God? Are you willing for God to show you areas where you need to be careful?

GROUP STUDY

- What are some of the traits of our Father that we can imitate?

- If Scripture and the Spirit are sources of light, what do you need to do to live in that light?

- Do you know someone who lives such a loving, sacrificial life that wherever he/she goes, it is as if he/she leaves a sweet fragrance behind?

- Most people try to hide things in their lives that they know are wrong. Have you ever tried to cover up a wrong and then had it discovered by someone? Describe the outcome.

- Why is it dangerous and unhealthy to try to cover up wrongs?

- Is there a person or a small group with whom you can develop a relationship or accountability as a means of helping you live carefully in light and love?

LIVING IN LOVING RELATIONSHIPS

LISTENING FOR GOD THROUGH EPHESIANS 5:21—6:9

Summary

The healthy Christian life that honors God will include healthy, loving relationships—particularly at home and at work. Healthy relationships must have an element of submission in them, the willingness to surrender some of each person's will and rights to that of the other person. Yet many people could not describe their home lives in these terms. Their experience is more like poor relationships that suck the joy out of life and heaven out of our spirit.

In the home, marriage is to be a reflection of Christ's love for the Church—filled with submissive, self-sacrificing love and respect. Healthy families also include children who obey and honor their parents and parents who do not exasperate their children.

In the workplace, similar principles apply. Workers have a responsibility to work and witness as if they were doing it for Christ, and employers have a responsibility to understand that they answer to God for the way they treat their workers.

PREPARATION ☦ FOCUS YOUR THOUGHTS

How does your family build memory moments? What great family moment comes to mind right now?

If you could fix one thing in your family, what would it be?

READING ☦ HEAR THE WORD

The first word in this section of Scripture is a hard one for some people to accept and harder to put into practice—*submit*. It means to voluntarily yield to the power and authority of another. If two people submit to each other, it means that there will be mutual respect, cooperation, and collaboration. There will be no abuse or manipulation.

The marriage relationship is modeled after Christ's love for the Church. Christ's love for the Church is to be a model of how a husband should love his wife. Wives are asked to submit to their husbands, but this does not give husbands control over their wives, because they are also to be submissive "out of reverence for Christ." Equally, husbands are commanded to love their wives with the sacrificial love of Christ.

Other words like *love, obey, honor, respect,* and *serve* are found throughout this instruction about relationships. The focus of a Christian in relationship is not upon self, but upon others.

The principle of God's way is that when you invest yourself

in others—family, friends, and coworkers—you'll experience the most joy.

Read Ephesians 5:21—6:9, looking for evidence of these truths.

MEDITATION ✝ ENGAGE THE WORD

Meditate on Ephesians 5:21-33

Submission is a choice—a willful decision to yield your rights to another. Why is that hard for most people to do?

Read the statement by Donald Kauffman. Do you agree with this perspective on marriage? What is the difference between a contract and a covenant?

> *A good marriage is not a contract between two persons but a sacred covenant between three. Too often Christ is never invited to the wedding and finds no room in the home.* —*Donald Kauffman*

Wives are to submit to their husbands "as to the Lord," and husbands are to love their wives "as Christ loved." How does this moderate the fear of control and domination?

The goal of Christ's love for the Church is revealed in verses 26-27. Within that is the goal that the Church be holy and blameless—the same goal for individuals that was mentioned in chapter 1. How can the Church, a collection of individuals in a wide range of spiritual development, be holy and blameless?

Meditate on Ephesians 6:1-4

Like *submit, obey* may be considered demeaning or restrictive. There can be something in the human spirit that resists both. What is right about children obeying their parents?

Do you agree with the statement made by the dying father? Why, or why not?

> *A dying Christian father said to his wife, "See that you bring the children up to honor and obey you, for if they don't obey you when they are young, they won't obey God when they are older."*

Verse 2 says honoring parents "is the first commandment with a promise." What is meant by this? What is the promise?

Fathers are specifically mentioned in verse 4, but mothers can be included as well. Parents are not to *exasperate* their children. What does exasperate mean? In what ways might parents exasperate their children?

Read the statement by Richard Milnes on page 67. How is your home to be the workshop of Christ? How are parents and children to work together to make this possible? How is God involved in this process?

> *The Christian home is the Master's workshop where the processes of character molding are silently, lovingly, faithfully and successfully carried on.*
>
> *—Richard Milnes*

Parenthood is a wonderful privilege with an awesome responsibility. Parents are not to passively watch their children grow up. They are to "bring them up," which suggests active involvement in the process of providing, nurturing, training, and instructing. What is the difference between training and instructing? How do you think a parent could provide the "training and instruction of the Lord"?

Meditate on Ephesians 6:5-9

Workers are to relate to their employers with obedience, respect, and sincerity. If you have ever had a job, what is the motivation for obeying requests of your employer? What should Christians do if their employers ask them to do things considered inappropriate? What if they are not the kind of people who can be respected?

Christian workers are to do their work as if they were obeying Christ, as if they were slaves of Christ, and as if they were serving the Lord. Do you look at your work (or schoolwork) that way?

Read the statement by Charles Stelzle. How can you take the common tasks that you must do and make them "immortal tasks"?

> *God never calls a lazy, disgruntled man to a job which requires the finer qualities of real manhood. Every worker may make the commonest job an immortal task.*
> *—Charles Stelzle*

PRAYER ☨ ASK AND LISTEN

Seek the face of God. Ask, "Lord, what are You saying to us today?"

People flourish when living and working within loving relationships. Who needs to experience an expression of your love? Pray and ask God to lead you to people with whom you can share the love of God.

CONTEMPLATION ☨ REFLECT AND YIELD

How would your world be different if people around you genuinely cared about each other? How could you be more caring? Are you willing to remove relational barriers that may exist in your life?

GROUP STUDY

- The basis for our submission to others is reverence for Christ. What connection does reverence for Christ have with our relationship to others?

- As you enter the time of transition between childhood and adulthood, what should you do about the command to children to obey their parents? Does this still apply to you?

- Think of one way you can honor your parent(s) this week. Will this be easy? Why, or why not?

- How can we serve others at home, school, and work like we are serving Christ?

- We are to be like Christ in our relationships and work as if we are working for Him. Make a list of changes you would like to see in the atmosphere of your home and your school. Name something you can do today to help change this atmosphere.

LIVING VICTORIOUSLY IN A HOSTILE WORLD

LISTENING FOR GOD THROUGH EPHESIANS 6:10-24

SUMMARY

Believers enjoy grace that has been lavished on them, along with all of the accompanying blessings. They have been lifted up into the heavenly realms in Christ. The problem is that they must live their new life in a world where they experience adversity and attacks by ungodly powers.

Living victoriously requires the following: recognizing the enemy, taking a committed stand, relying on the strength of God, putting on the protective gear that is available, and praying about your battles. The great thing about these requirements is that each one comes directly from the hand of God.

Paul closes out this rich letter with thoughts about others. He could have talked about the difficulties he was facing in prison, but he simply asked for prayer that he would be fearless and effective in his witness. He wanted to finish well. A bit of heaven filled his cell and caused life in a hostile world to still be purposeful, endurable, and victorious. He wrote this section so the same could be true of you, regardless of what imprisons you or what adversity you may be facing.

PREPARATION ✝ FOCUS YOUR THOUGHTS

For what do you most often pray? Do you pray as much for others as you do for yourself? If you could improve your prayer practices, what would you most like to change?

READING ✝ HEAR THE WORD

The cosmic war between good and evil—God and Satan—is sometimes found raging in our personal worlds. The battle may be fought internally or externally, with physical or spiritual adversaries, or with persons or circumstances. A common result of living in a fallen world is that we must deal with temptations, adversity, illnesses, trauma, relational conflict, doubts, and resistance to our commitments.

Here, Paul identifies some of life's adversaries and the way to appropriate the power of God so you can be strong and stand. This isn't heaven; bad things happen to you, but your relationship with Christ and His Spirit residing within you can help you overcome the struggle.

Read Ephesians 6:10-24. Note how frequently the word *stand* occurs. Standing is portrayed as the posture of the person who is strong in the power of God.

MEDITATION ☩ ENGAGE THE WORD

Meditate on Ephesians 6:10-13

What sources of conflict does Paul identify? What do you understand these to be?

One of your adversaries is identified as the devil who is scheming against you. Who is the devil? What attributes and powers does he possess?

God has made adequate provision for you to be able to stand against the schemes of the devil. What provision does He offer? What is your responsibility in the deal?

In the quote below, Aaron Hill suggests that trials can have a valued effect in our lives. In what way? Do you agree with what he says?

> *There is no merit where there is no trial; and until experience stamps the mark of strength, cowards may pass for heroes, and faith for falsehood.*
>
> —*Aaron Hill*

Meditate on Ephesians 6:13-17

Reflect on how Paul uses the word *stand* and what he might mean by each use.

The armor of God is identified in these verses. What is the importance of each piece for a Christian's protection and powerful living? What must you do to put on each piece of armor?

The quote by John Greenleaf Whittier echoes Paul's insights about the believer's struggles. How do his words compare to your resolve?

So let it be in God's own might
We gird us for the coming fight,
And, strong in Him whose cause is ours
In conflict with unholy powers,
We grasp the weapons
He has given,—
The Light and Truth, and Love of Heaven.

—John Greenleaf Whittier

Meditate on Ephesians 6:18-20

There were those who thought they could silence Paul and curtail his ministry by placing him in prison. Paul referred to himself as "an ambassador in chains." What did he mean by this?

Paul did not pray for freedom from prison, but rather for freedom to proclaim the gospel without fear. Do people more often pray for a resolution to their problem or for the ability to honor God and fulfill their purpose in spite of their problem?

As Fred Beck indicates below, our power to stand is directly related to our reliance upon God. Prayer is a blessed privilege. It is also a critical necessity. How does Beck's challenge come into play in your own life circumstances?

> *If you are swept off your feet, it's time to get on your knees.* *—Fred Beck*

We are strengthened by prayer—our prayers to God on our own behalf and the prayers of others on our behalf. What are you doing to cultivate both kinds of prayers?

Read the quote from Phillips Brooks. What is he suggesting about the focus of our prayers as we face the adversities of life? Can you see yourself praying in this way? Why, or why not?

> *O, do not pray for easy lives. Pray to be stronger men. Do not pray for tasks equal to your powers. Pray for powers equal to your tasks.* *—Phillips Brooks*

Meditate on Ephesians 6:21-24

We are strengthened through the relationships we have that speak words of encouragement, faith, and love to us. Whom has God placed in your life that encourages you?

It is important that we be sensitive to the situations others are facing and be supportive of them. What means do you have of being made aware of the needs of others so you can encourage them and pray for them?

Paul's closing includes powerful words—*peace, love, faith,* and *grace*—that he speaks into the lives of these friends. Our words have the power to lift up or tear down.

Robert Hawker's benedictory prayer is a fitting way to conclude the study of Ephesians. It reflects the spirit of Paul as he closes his letter to believers who live in a world that can be hostile but whose life in Christ and in the church helps them be victorious. How can you see yourself, with God's strength, triumphing in redeeming love?

> *Lord, dismiss us with thy blessing,*
> *Hope, and comfort from above;*
> *Let us each, thy peace possessing,*
> *Triumph in redeeming love.*
>
> —*Robert Hawker*

PRAYER ✝ ASK AND LISTEN

Seek the face of God. Ask, "Lord, what are You saying to us today?"

Tell God about a situation in your life that has become a battlefield. Allow His Spirit to calm your spirit, bring peace to your mind, and reveal the means for living in His power and protection.

CONTEMPLATION ✝ REFLECT AND YIELD

How could you more effectively incorporate a pattern of spiritual discipline in your life of prayer, Bible reading, worship, quietness, meditation, and witness? Are you willing to do the things that will make you stronger and more able to live victoriously?

GROUP STUDY

- Paul indicates that our strength to overcome comes from God. How can you use God's power in your life so you can be spiritually strong?

- In what ways might the devil scheme against you? What do *you* do to fight against him?

- Is there a particular piece of armor that has proven effective and meaningful in your experience? Is there a piece that you may be missing?

- In what ways do you cultivate the practice of speaking words into the lives of people near you? Do your words uplift these people?

- God wants you to be strong in the face of hostile influences in the world. List two areas of your life where you could be most susceptible to temptation. Name at least one thing you are going to begin doing today that will keep you strong when experiencing temptation.

- How has the message of Ephesians changed your life?